re•viv•al

When Dead Bones Sing Again

J.J. Allen

contents

introduction: The Walking DEAD.   5

chapter one: The RIVER.   19
chapter two: THERE IS AN OUTPOUR.   37
chapter three: BURNING FIELDS   63
chapter four: POWER!   79
chapter five: MANIFESTING WONDERS.   95

acknowledgements   131
about the author   133

introduction

The Walking DEAD.

Something is happening. The earth and the people that dwell are in distress. People are dying. Preachers are without God. People are without hope. There's rebellion at an unprecedented level, and the tolerance for the profane has become our normal. Something has died. There is a loss somewhere deep down in the heart of humanity.

Remembering the Holy Time.

I love God, I love His church, and I love His mysteries. But if I may be honest for a bit…I dread some of our western cultural expression of "The Kingdom." As a kid, I often hated "youth church" because I felt like they'd throw cookies, juice boxes, and a few games our way while the adults were upstairs getting to encounter a raw manifestation of HIS power. I grew up in a church and within a community of believers, that while not perfect, strived to see the heart of God demonstrated and made alive.

I remember seeing the power of God demonstrated in services long before we had YouTube, Instagram praise break clips, and Facebook live. Nothing wrong with any of that, but I remember a time where we focused on the moment verses reaching for a device. Sunday morning service would start at 8 am followed by Sunday school at 10 am, 12 noon service, and Sunday night. Tuesdays we'd have bible study at 7:30 pm and Fridays were, "Evangelistic Night", usually the night where a fiery preacher would get up and set the hearts and souls of those present ablaze. It was my favorite service throughout the week, to be honest.

Services would start off long before the program would begin. I remember, many days walking into church hearing the audio recordings of Bishop C.H. Mason being played throughout the building. That would end and for another 15-20 minutes, "the saints" as we called them, would walk around the church, praying, clapping, and glorifying God. Many of my childhood examples of prayer have since crossed the river, but even as I write I can hear them praying and the repetitious sounds of intercession and thanksgiving. I think about Elder George Blackwell, a godly older man. He would walk and work at the same time. Often you could find him walking around the church making sure things were in order, speaking to the saints in between his three claps, chanting, "Glorrrrry, Glory,

Glory" (clap, clap, clap). It was music to my ears.

Mother Pearl Baldwin, is the epitome of an intercessor. I mean, a classical Pentecostal watchmen fluent in provoking the presence of the Lord. I would often as a kid hear her crying, "JESUS!" No matter the worship moment, no matter how long it lasted, she would call on HIS name in a melodious chant that would be both sweet and powerful at the same time.

The long lasting lingering times in HIS presence are some of the most unforgettable moments to me. EVER. I think I grew up on the dying tail end of the church without schedule. Church ended when it ended as a kid. I could almost never tell you what time we were going to get out, and often it seemed silly when someone inquired about what time church would be over. We waited in HIS presence. It never took the Spirit long to make Himself known, but what I often appreciated and what was instilled in me was to acknowledge that He was present, appreciate the moment, and not to disrespect HIM by rushing out of it. We weren't afraid to linger because of after-church hobbies.

As a kid, "convocation/convention season" was everything to me. It was days of the presence of God; night after night with different speakers, different demonstrations, and different sounds but all under one NAME. I was blessed to drink from the river of God. Convocation was a time where the saints would gather from all over, various churches and communities of believers would gather in one place. They would fly in, drive in, some would even come from around the corner. It was the gathering of people you would really only see but sometimes, maybe once a year. It was a great time of fellowship.

We would have these intense moments in the Spirit, and often times, it came from yelling men and women who weren't even on the pulpit, program, or had special "ranking" in church. The power of God would come in like waves, and most times, we were sensitive enough to ride them. Many times, the preacher would stand after a moment of exhortation, and out of nowhere, one of the saints, one in particular Sis. Simmons, would come from Holy Temple, and without fail, we'd hear the speaking of tongues from her or at times another. I mean, they could be in the back of a packed church, and within a few moments, the entire church would become silent.

There was a reverence and respect for the word of God being present. At times, she would speak and then interpret what the Lord was speaking to His people, or we experienced moments where after one would speak, another would come from no where and stand up, and began to speak, "thus saith the Lord, for yea I am God..." and would speak in authority under a pure anointing. Everyone would work in sync, and when the moment was over, they went back to being unheard and unseen.

I'm no old man. I'm not writing as one recalling precious memories from 60 years ago. I was just born at the end of one culture, groomed in the spirit of one, and being used by God at the end of another. I have seen the Glory. I have touched the Glory. I have experienced God in ways I don't think I can write and still be looked at as "normal." But in all of that, I realize that my moments but drops of what Heaven has prepared for the hungry of NOW. There is always MORE, and never a shortage of power.

Something Died.

I write from a very strange place. It's strange because I'm frustrated, yet excited. I'm hungry, but I'm tired. I want to see God, but I don't want to. There has to be more. I studied church history, Pentecostal/Charismatic movements throughout the world for some years. I studied many of the figureheads, generals, and movements and as a teen that put such a hunger in me. In my heart, I've always known that there had to be more than what I have seen. Where is this power? Where are these gifts? Did it all die? Has God finished with demonstrating His power in unprecedented ways? What has happened to the church? Please understand, I'm not referring to the diversity or gifts. I understand that not all will be the same in demonstration. I'm also aware of times and seasons. Some movements were graced for certain moments in time. All of those things are understood.

My heart's plea and burden however, is for the altar that's been forsaken. I grieve for the wells that have no water. We're building bigger churches, and our communities of faiths are becoming more advanced, influential, and we are really doing great things. But something is missing. There has to be more to God than just coming to church, having a religious experience and then going back home to live your life—only to come back week by week and repeat. It's a brand of Christianity I'm just not interested in. I don't want it. I don't want to live it, and I don't want to preach it. I don't want to fellowship with it. I want the power of God and I want Him real in my life.

As a kid, prayer wasn't seen as a *movement,* as it was something that came naturally. There were no flyers that had to be made to engage believers to fast. God called holy times for His people to be set apart, and those that were HIS, obeyed. What has happened to the church? I'm in no way judging. My heart's desire is to plead for the purity in our passion. I dream of people that pursue after God simply because they love Him. I love God and I want everyone I encounter to fall in love with HIM too.

I sit at times, and I watch people go to church, preach a gospel, and not be convicted or inspired to change by the very gospel they preach. This is bigger than sin. Often times I think we focus so much on sin and being "okay" because what we are doing isn't in the bible. This is about a dying heart. This is about vain imaginations, twisted passions, and our lack of pursuit. God is west, we are north, and we have become content with where we are.

We've become bigger in enterprise but very small in power. We have the money, we have grandeur, we have everything you can possibly need to be successful in a modern age. The church has no doubt come a very long way visibly, especially for charismatic people. We're on primetime t.v. with entertainers, and I don't believe everyone has compromised to get there. I believe that there are some amazing God representatives that are bringing recognition to Christ in the culture. Please understand, this is not a jab at the bride. I don't believe in bashing the church. As a church and a people of faith, we've come along way from the first century believers who merely worshipped in houses.

I ask one thing in all of this. Is God finished? If what happened in the days of old, will never return, cool. If what I experienced and seen in my childhood days are gone, okay. I can live with that. I could exist and be okay, shifting as long as God was shifting with me. I've done my best to be "normal." I look at how the modern preachers are supposed to dress. I've studied their brands, and I have tried an array of changes over the course of my ministry.

No one wants to feel like an odd duck, out of place, or the "super deep person". But I have kept silent when inwardly HE was screaming, "LET ME OUT!". I looked at what was trendy and what was popular and I tried to see myself through the eyes of it. In the midst of it all, I kept finding myself growing more frustrated and disappointed because none of it was working.

No conference I attended seemed to do the trick. I kept looking for something that I could not find, and to be honest I didn't even know what I was looking for. All I know was, I kept doing what I knew to do and I kept feeling empty. I would find myself going through mundane fasts, hearing generic preacher and prophecy, living in an afterglow of a childhood experience and I was dying.

In my quest to fit in, I silenced my conviction. That conviction however, I can silence no more. I look around, and I'm convinced, this ain't it. This is not that church that the Apostles contended for. We've built mega brands, but have forsaken the altar. The old church didn't have much…but they had GOD. William Seymour did more with one eye, than many of us have done with 20,000 followers. They had faith, they had pursuit, they had smoke.

I see dead bones singing.

I went through a phase where I was out of compassion. I wished evil on no one, but to me, everyone would receive the consequences of their actions…myself included. I was tired of preaching and praying for people that seemingly would go and do whatever they wanted to do. I said God, this just isn't working. I quit. I was a little bitter and angry because, though I said I didn't care, I found myself caring too much. It was then that the Lord showed me myself and allowed me to see pride and frustration in operation.

When God gives you the ability to see the dead,

that's not your time to weep and talk about "what use to be" and share memories. That's the time to prophesy! I was so engulfed with my own emotions, that I didn't realize that He was giving me a chance to see the coming glory…once again. Only God can make dead things come alive again. He turns hopeless, rejected, and lifeless things into beautiful marks of honor for HIS glory.

What good is it to have eyes and can't see? What benefit does it serve you to have a mouth and cannot speak? YES! There's been a great death. Things have changed. There is much that we can see through the cracks and chips of our faith within our church. Don't be robbed of a valley called beautiful that's before your eyes. Our wicked world has given God something to work with. God is up to something amazing.

These dead bones will live again. We will sing a new song unto HIM for what He has done. It will be the ultimate song of redemption. God will condition our heart for the culture that's to come. And fathers will walk with sons, priests will sing with laity, mothers will dance with daughters…and we will all ascend unto the holy hill of the Lord, singing "life music" in the river of God. We'll stand in the middle of river singing, "Death has no victory, heaven has no sorrow, God did it. He won again. I was dead, but I'm alive again."

chapter one

THE RIVER.

There is a river that makes glad the city of God, the holy
place, where the Most High lives.
-Psalms 46: 4

He that believeth on Me, as the scripture hath said, 'out
of his belly shall flow rivers of living water.'
-John 7:38

There was a hymn I often heard as a kid, it simply said:
I've got a river of life flowing out of me

Makes the lame to walk and the blind to see

Open prison doors, set the captive free

I've got a river of life, flowing out of me.

Spring up O well, down in my soul…

Spring up o well, and make me whole…

Spring up O well, and give to me, that life abundantly

I am most fulfilled in the river. I make songs, melodies within my heart in this river. It is the source of my strength, the source of my life—the RIVER is my lifeline. Even as I write, I fight to contain my excitement and passion. It was in the river, that I received the abundance of my revelation. The river is where I was healed. From the river of God is where I have been nourished and given water in great times of spiritual famine. It's cleaned me. It's washed me. And what I think is so amazing above all of that is that it dwells in me.

For years, I struggled to be a carrier of the glory and a proclaimer of the gospel. Flaws and insecurities have often kept me feeling less than. Sins and mistakes of the past kept me fearful of moving forward. But all of that cease to matter in the river! I gained my confidence and take solace in the fact that I've got a river in me. What causes me not to be envious of the gift of friends is the fact that in me is living water! I've got a well down in my soul that springs forth life. EVERYWHERE I GO, EVERYTHING I TOUCH, there will be revival, why? Because the river is in me.

I believe my greatest call isn't to prophesy, preach to masses, or write books. I take great pleasure and become aggressive in seeing the river stirred within the souls of men. If I can cause the wells in the belly of dead men to spring forth, I have served God well in my assignment.

THERE IS A RIVER. I believe that God is extending the invitation for the world at large to come and be partakers of the RIVER. Many are gathered for different reasons, but I believe most widely, He's beckoning all those willing to take a dip.

CLEANSING.

Then Naaman went down and dipped himself in the Jordan seven times, according to the command of the man of God: and his flesh came again like unto the flesh of a little child, and he was clean.

-II Kings 5:14

There was a horrible epidemic in the land called leprosy. This diseased caused many to be sick, cast out, mocked, shunned and left to suffer alone. No help, and no assistance, those that were afflicted had visible proof of this affliction and could not hide their flaws. Leprosy was the great plague of the day. It was a disease that affected the body at large. The hands, the feet, the face, even to the deterioration of nerves. I think what is perhaps the most grueling thing about it was it's ability to be present, and have no physical pain as a sign of your condition. It eats away at the ability to sense pain due to the nerve damage over time.

With any sickness, we know or often have some sort of warning signs that lead us to seek help. We get achy, start coughing, and congested. Our discomfort and pain leads us to know that there is something that needs to be checked out. Unfortunately, those with leprosy didn't have it that way. They had no pain to point them to help. It's one thing to be afflicted, it's completely different when your affliction has desensitized to the pain. You can't even recognize when you're hurting or in serious danger. We cry and we run from pain, but pain can save your life. Pain is a sign that you're still alive. Only the dead feel no pain. It's so important that we watch for the things we grow cold and numb to overtime.

Second Kings tells the story of a man named Naaman. He was a leader and someone of notoriety. This man of great stature came in contact with this infirmity. The bible tells it this way, "…he was a mighty man of valor, but he was a leper." (II Kings 5:1) As great as he was, he was summed up by his infirmity. Isn't it astonishing that all of the clout, recognition, nor power could keep him from being infected? ***Even leaders battle to be whole.*** Something happens to Naaman that doesn't happen often in this period of time. They send for a prophet by the name of Elisha to come and cleanse Naaman of this disease. Elisha doesn't even go to Naaman himself, but sends the word back to him that in order to be cleansed, he had to go wash in the Jordan River. Naaman becomes full of pride and self-righteous wanting to be cleansed his way.

As I examine a lot of what's going on within our world, I see people that want to be healed, but be healed their way. Even among our leaders, there is a need for revival and refreshing, but we're too proud to come to the river that God has assigned for our deliverance. Yes, you're the pastor. Yes, you're an amazing gift, but maybe the river God has for you might be you becoming undignified in the company of the people. Perhaps you as the head of your house need to call a fast, and everyone see you on your needs praying and waiting before the Lord.

Naaman's pride almost caused him to stay in his condition. Everyone didn't get healed. Everyone wasn't given instructions to go to the river. What made Naaman stand out was his willingness to inquire of a holy man. It's in our pursuit of the Holy MAN that we receive our invitation to "COME!" Naaman was the only one during the time of Elisha the prophet to be healed (see Luke 4:27). There were many that were sick, but only the one that washed in the river was made whole. Are you willing to get out of your norm, break your routine, and allow God to cleanse you thoroughly? REVIVAL awaits the man with clean hands.

REFRESHING.

Repent therefore, and reform your lives, so that the record of your sins may be cancelled, and that there may come seasons of revival from the Lord.

-Acts 3:19 (WNT)

Things happen. In this journey, we get a few bumps and bruises along the way. You can be at war, and go through seasons of great battle, and at times, need to be refreshed. Remember Samson? When he was fighting and defeated a thousand Philistines with the jawbone of an ass, he cried out to God, that he was thirsty, and it was the Lord who opened up the hallow places where he stood causing fresh water to flow out of it (Judges 15:19).

God will call us to the river as a time to be refreshed. Some times, it's not about cleansing, sometimes it's about preservation. God wants you to be sustained in your journey. He doesn't want you having to cope with drugs, and turning to things that will interfere with your perception. God never meant for crying yourself to sleep at night to be the remedy to your battles. There is a well of refreshing, and it's available for those that will come.

Repent, change your ways, and all that you've done

will be forgotten. The well is a byproduct of HIS grace and not your works. Nothing you do will satisfy the thirsting of your soul. God invites you to the river that you may be whole.

Serving God while being burnt-out is only acceptable for a season. While it's never God's plan or desire, it happens. But we're not to stay in this condition. Service to God should never be a burden. If you find it increasingly difficult to worship, pray, go to church, or just live life and enjoy it, you may just be in a drought. If nothing is working---you may very well be empty. You need fresh water.

Get out of your own way, turn to God, and experience a season of revival. THERE. IS. LIFE.

RULES OF REFRESHING.

- ***Don't routine the Holy Spirit.*** No two flows are ever the same. Maybe the power of God came in on a certain song one Sunday; that doesn't mean it's the model song.

- *Be open.* A closed mind will never experience the reward of HIS presence. Allow The SPIRIT to lead. Let Him guide and do as HE desires. You must be of the mind that says, "anything can happen". He knows what He's doing, and you have to be alright with whatever He's doing in the moment. Be sensitive as to yield the moment to HOLY SPIRIT.

- *Be discerning.* Not every spirit is of God. Some prophesy, speak in tongues, do all sorts of emotional things out of the mere flesh. Don't embrace everything that looks like "a move of God." Everything doesn't require a dance, and everything doesn't require a shout. Be discerning of spirits that come to mock and deceive even in the midst of the congregation.

- ***Be patient.*** While we don't have to "tarry" and plead for HOLY SPIRIT to come and abide, it makes an amazing "thank you" to HIM when we don't rush out of HIS presence. Bask, linger, and enjoy HIM.

- ***Stop*** asking for God to, "show up" and when He manifests with great signs you don't know what to do, so you attempt to control it and go back to your routine.

- ***Let HIM flow.*** Sing songs in the spirit. Don't contain or try to fight what He does in you. There are moments I find myself jumping out of my sleep in the Spirit. Yielding to HIM, I'll holler out in my heavenly language, I'll raise my hands, and mutter in the unknown, sometimes in a song—and I will go back to sleep right after. I don't question it anymore, I don't attempt to not do it. I allow the rivers of revival to flow, that HE may be glorified. In me I want no hindrances, I want no blockage. All I want is a steady stream. You see, for me, it is easy to publically demenstrate HIM, because in private, I routinely practice loving HOLY SPIRIT. We live consistent in private, so in public, what people call being, "anointed" really isn't that at all. You're only seeing a public display of what we do privately.

MANY STREAMS, ONE RIVER...

Now there are diversities of gifts, but the same Spirit. And there are differences of administrations, but the same Lord. And there are diversities of operations, but it is the same God which worketh all in all. But the manifestation of the Spirit is given to every man to profit withal.

-I Corinthians 12: 4-7 KJV

Each person is given something to do that shows who God is: Everyone gets in on it, everyone benefits. All kinds of things are handed out by the Spirit, and to all kinds of people.

V. 7 (MGS)

I think one of the greatest wars against the church is the division within the church. It's my observation that we demonize what we don't understand. Once upon a time, those that spoke in tongues were mocked, seen as unintelligent, and lower-than because of their acts. Baptists and other denominations weren't saved because they didn't speak in tongues. Growing up, I've heard people say some wild things about others within the church.

You weren't saved if you wore pants. In my culture, if you didn't yell, hold your ear, and preach with some sort of music, you were considered boring. You weren't filled with the Spirit if you didn't dance in church. "Black church" had more "Holy Ghost" than the "white church." In modern culture, we debate and say that CCM and Hillsong are more anointed than Gospel and Hymns. We bicker over things and make doctrines out of preference when in fact, no where in the bible is concrete foundation for our overzealous convictions.

I have seen some outrageous things in the name of "The Spirit" and conviction. But the reality is the bible says quite the opposite of what we tend to bash others for. I admit, I've always been a bit of a wild man. Thankfully, I grew up in a church that exposed me to various styles and types of ministries. I've seen both boring yellers, and mesmerizing talkers. I would always be drawn to different administrations of gifting. I would go to both Hispanic worship services and West Indian worship services. I've been to prayer meetings with the Foursquare, and I've been to bible study with the Presbyterian. I've cried with the Lutheran, and I have preached for the Methodist.

All expressions of Jesus to me are beautiful. In relations to gifts, as a kid growing up in Pentecost, I would see people operate in great power, and I would sit, marveling with the promise to myself, "one day, I'm going to preach like that". I won't lie to you, the first time I preached and someone fell out in the spirit and prophecy manifested in a rather heavy manner, I was shocked and humbled…but felt like God had used me greatly because someone fell out. I was operating out of my shell, and yelling, and prophesying, and doing all of these wonderful works of Jesus, and I thought, THIS IS POWER!

As time progressed, and as I began to mature a bit more in my gifts (as I am even still), I went through a very intense time where I seen God use me in the prophetic. I mean, every service, every moment, I would prophesy the Word of the Lord. Words of knowledge, words of wisdom, I would speak in clarity to people, churches, and primarily leaders as I was permitted. When that phase ceased, I realized that while I was able to still prophesy…I spent much time teaching. Some of my greatest messages of deliverance came through teaching. It was as if the word came alive and did the work. No altar calls, no laying on of hands, no personal prophecy…but I just taught the word of the Lord….and people were delivered.

At one point in my life, I was begging God to operate in me more. I was trying my best to preach hard and do everything I thought demonstrated power, and the Lord helped me to see that it wasn't about me and my need to feel important, it was about what was needed at that moment so that true deliverance could happen. I gained so much from that. It changed my perspective.

I'll never discredit another gift. It may be packaged in a way I don't understand. I may not get it, I may not even agree with it, however, if it is led by The Spirit, my opinion and my thoughts aren't needed. Maybe the common won't work at that moment. Maybe God needs a different type of gift. All gifts. All souls belong to God. Don't despise the gifts you don't understand. It may be completely unlike anything you've ever seen before, but be okay with what God is doing. Don't say you love Jesus, and kill His creativity at the same time.

Some yell, some sing, some dance, others pray…very long. Some prophesy, some work miracles, some use prayer cloths as points of contact, some hold healing lines, some preach on healing for hours until people are whole. Some fast 30 days and some are just weird. I'm one of those weird guys. Fact is, there are many streams. If everyone prophesies the same, dance the same, and worship the same…you're not in harmony, you're in a cult. The RIVER is filled with many styles you know not of. EMBRACE IT.

No man owns the river. It moves, and it flows freely. Just when you think it's going in one direction, the wind can blow, and water can come gushing over rock that you didn't even expect to get wet. God has ways, areas, and spaces that you've never even considered. He's not coming back the same.

There are gifts unwrapped and ministries untold. No gift is greater than another, but diverse for sure. Expand your capacity to receive. REVIVAL exposes the heart of originality. God promotes what looks like Him and sounds like Him that haven't been mimicked yet. He's intentional in manifesting in ways we've never seen. Let's consider: could it be that the cries of the angels one to another, "Holy, Holy, Holy" as recorded in scripture, isn't because that's all they know to say, but because when they behold Him, they see a different dimension of Him that they've yet to see before? There are sides, depths, and levels to His Holiness that we will never fully comprehend. I imagine that to behold Him and blink is to see again a newness in HIM that you've never seen before. To behold HIS manifestation through others is a display of HIS genius and creative nature.

chapter two

THERE IS AN OUTPOUR.

outpour
to flow out rapidly; to pour out.

> And it shall come to pass in the last days, says God,
> That I will pour out of My Spirit on all flesh;
> That I will pour out of My Spirit on all flesh;
> Your sons and your daughters shall prophesy,
> Your young men shall see visions,
> Your old men shall dream dreams.
> -Acts 2:17NKJV

It's not uncommon for catchphrases, buzzwords, and trendy sayings to replace divine moments. In fact, I believe the idolatry of trends is what kills impartation. You can't receive from what you perceive as common. The dangerous thing of trends is that while it may be relevant and great to capitalize on at the moment, it will lose its potency and vitality as we all treat it as, "just another word". "REVIVAL". I have been hearing that term forever. All of my life, I've heard that we were in the last days and that God was going to pour His spirit out, and that the sons and daughters would prophesy. I've heard it at every youth conference, I've seen it on hundreds of flyers and in sermon notes. I've heard it, I've preached it. We all have. But it wasn't until the last year that the power of the word really began to do something different in me.

Closing out of 2017 was rough for me. I experienced many highs and many lows. More lows than highs, but all in all, a good year. As customary, the Lord often speaks in relation to what the new year's theme and focus for my life, ministry, and direction will be. In the past few years, because of my own decisions and because of just life, I've lost a lot, I've learned a lot, and I just grew as a man. In my faith, in my walk, I experienced things that challenged me. I'll be the first to admit, as much as I've recovered and healed, I lost some hope along the way. I put some dreams down. I let some promises go. Some things I prayed and believed God for, I got to a place where I would say, "maybe, not for me." When you go through war, you learn to be content with just being out, you don't do too much begging for old things.

Something in me died along the way. If I was going to experience this holy revival to come, I was going to have to admit my reality. I believed God and believed that it could happen for everyone else but me. I knew God could and would heal the bodies of others, and I believed Him to perform the word that He'd spoke over the lives of His people, but I just didn't think He'd do it for me anymore. I was serving God and merely happy just serving Him.

After all of the mistakes and things I'd done, while I would never admit it, every so often, I found myself living to work for God to make up for the things I done. I didn't want to ask for much, because I didn't think I deserved it. I messed up, and thought that it forfeited my rights and access to my inheritance.

I'd have some pretty sparadic days spiritually. Some seasons, I found myself trying to fast and operate like I knew how, and though a measure of the anointing would be present, it wasn't the same as before. There's nothing worse than operating under a cloud that left two seasons ago. I had to repent and become honest with God. I was frustrated because my prayers weren't working. I was preaching and prophesying, but there was no rain. Sure, there was a mist and movement but what I knew of God, was not present. I was operating out of a moment of grace, instead of a well. The well within my soul was dry. I needed a refreshing! I needed a reviving. I was tired of church experiences where I couldn't really go fully into

HIM all the time because I was the preacher or because it was cut short to move on in the service.

I wanted God to pour HIS Spirit upon me afresh. I found myself listening to everyone's ministry clips and tapes trying to see if it would stir something within me, and as anointed as they were, it didn't do it. I would go to various things, and while they were anointed events and services, it didn't last for me. It was as if I would get filled up just enough to the next attack, and I would lose the little water that I had. I was ministering and living out of the "reserved tank". I no longer had the desire to study His word. I no longer had the desire to seek Him the way that I used to. God and I didn't talk how we use to talk at 4 am. I missed the seasons where He would wake me up in the middle of the night, and it would feel as though He would tap me and start talking. I'm talking about supernatural moments with HIM. I missed it all. And I didn't know how to get back to it.

I have a few friends, who will rename nameless for

story sake. They'll tell you with pride that they will NEVER fill their gas tank up. They can have a pocket full of money, but $5 here for gas or $15 there. There is no priority in filling up the tank. There's always just enough to get to where they have to get to and then, go get a refill. And it works for them. That's like many of us. I know me, myself personally, it was. I found myself serving in my church, trying to work a full time job, and trying to build in HIS name, without being filled. I was trying to build my life, keep the kid a priority, and build a ministry all on empty. I was in a space where I would get filled just enough to get me to where I was going. I would have just enough to preach the next service. I had years of being filled "just enough". I spent a season living out of a reserve instead of the well within. And that season often led me into depression and brokenness. I wanted God and I knew there was more, but I was empty.

It was an emptiness that a "praise break" couldn't fix. Prophecy and someone laying hands on me couldn't solve. There was a refreshing that my soul longed for. I became unsatisfied with everything. Nothing was doing "the trick."

One day, The Spirit spoke to me so strongly, "REVIVAL!". Immediately, everything in me leaped. Going into 2017, He'd spoke in the similar manner concerning the year and said, "HELP!" He spoke of how He would send divine help, help from strangers, and help from people that didn't come with strings attached. True enough, throughout the year, help came in unconventional ways. I was merely grateful for divine assistance in my life, and didn't too much ask or even think about old prayers too much. So when He said, "REVIVAL" I was overwhelmed with joy.

He said, "if you commit to doing it MY way, if you will but become as a dead man without a fight, I'll resurrect everything your hands touch this year. This will be the year that dead things come alive again. The Resurrection has come." It took me into the new year in total astonishment. Before the end of winter, He not only resurrected a promise, but a 27 year wait of healing, manifested in my body. The RESSURECTION had come. REVIVAL was no longer coming. REVIVAL…was here. In me. It was then that I realized, revival wasn't some sort of public event, revival was in fact Christ alive in the heart again. I noticed when I opened my mouth, the song of the Lord would flow again, my preaching was met with power again. There was a renewal even in my capacity to understand the Scripture. My prayer life was set ablaze again. I was revived.

REVIVAL IS ________

I had a MAJOR revelation of what REVIVAL looked like. Growing up, when I heard the term, it would be used to describe a service that was unexplainable or at times just highly emotional. If we danced a lot, we called it revival. If we praised God a lot, we called it revival. We are in a moment in time where we plan a string of services and call them "revival" when in fact it's not. Revival for many of our contemporary churches is nothing short of a sanctified fundraiser. We pride ourselves on "going in" when the Spirit of God comes in great magnitude, and we allow ourselves to be free in HIS presence. But that's not the true mark of REVIVAL. The true mark, is being able to abide. STAYING IN THE SPIRIT. LIVING IN THE SPIRIT. GROWING WITH THE SPIRIT. REVIVAL is a way of life. No one experiences a holy revival and returns back to normalcy. It changes you forever.

When I think about revival, I think about a builder. I think about those used by God to do outrageous, courageous, and ridiculous things long before it made sense. Revival looks like:

- Moses in Egypt

- Noah building an ark.

- Samuel in the courts of Eli

- Ezekiel in the Valley of Dry Bones declaring that

there will be life again.

- Jonah in the belly of the whale

- Ninevah

- Jesus in the temple exclaiming, "the Spirit of the Lord is upon me, and He's anointed me to preach the gospel."

- John the Baptist in the wilderness, preparing the way of the Lord.

REVIVAL is work. Revival is passion. Revival is blood and tears. Revival is God's response to people that cry out. REVIVAL is the science of creation. It is the announcement of new life, an act of God's love, and the proof of HIS power. He makes dead things live again.

I am REVIVAL. I once was dead, but I'm alive again, because The Resurrection lives in ME. (John 11:26) So you see, it's much bigger than a Spring call or Summer event. REVIVAL is a spirit/culture. To be revived is to be armed again. God renews the spirit within and gives power to the faint. Revival is when God moves the stone away from a dead, stinky, wrapped up, and notably lifeless thing, and tells it to come forth because IT WILL LIVE AGAIN.

BUILD IT

REVIVAL. It is a promise that He gave us: LIFE. Interesting enough however, it's one of those paradoxes of Christianity. In essence, in order for something to be revived it has to first be dead. You have to lose something in order to gain something better. Sometimes a "loss" is not as a result of sin or doing anything wrong, but a reality that somehing has run its course. We lose strength along the way. We war, and at times, though we have faith, some defeats can cause us to lose hope. Dying is just a part of the process. Some things you believed in the infancy of your salvation, and the fire you had when you first got saved, you can admit, as years have gone by, you're not as on fire as you were.

Every so often, God shocks the heart of man, bringing the beat of HIS heart back. Our life is HIS life, and HIS life in us is what we are here for. What are you living out in HIS name?

REVIVAL must be built. It is not something that happens by chance. It is the result of people that war for it (we'll discuss that a little later.). It's hard work and labor that goes into a true move of the Spirit. Do the work both on earth and in the spirit that makes way for the habitation of heaven. In order to be a builder of revival, you must become like John the Baptist. You must be content in being one that simply prepares the way of the Lord. Be okay making way for the move of the Spirit to come. Do the ground work, plow, make ready, war for the Spirit of Revival.

I think many of the challenges we see in trying to stir revival is our ego. Not always in a boastful or prideful way, but we can become so used to doing everything, that we think, it's going to be OUR song, OUR church, OUR movement that's going to be the "IN" thing for the season. So, we focus so much on building US, that we don't foster relationships, we invest everything back into self, and we try to assist God in ways He just may not need help in. We are NOT the wonder. We are NOT the glory.

We are ALL vessels. Some have different responsibilities but nevertheless, every person has a spot in preparation. Building and builders matter. The one with the hammer is as much as important as the person with the paint. Every major move of The Spirit was birthed out of building. Revival goes through building stages. Building is the science of Manifestation. Nothing just happens.

S T A G E S   O F   B U I L D I N G.

The STIRRING.

REVIVAL is one of those things that can cause you to grow weary in your pursuit to see it. It's not one for those things you pray for once a week and then it happens the next Sunday. No sir, no ma'am. There are people who prayed for decades to see the supernatural released.

The one thing that you MUST have in order to see an authentic move of the Spirit is an appetite for it. There will be times you pray, and go to church weekly for a season and see little to no results of that. There will be moments where it looks as if your efforts to bring about change to your region, city, or church will go unnoticed. Things will seemingly look worst for a season. Prayer ministry and passion to worship will seem rather faint in the local church. Don't give up.

Those that hunger and thirst will be filled. Don't take the easy way out, don't settle for crumbs, and mere "touches from God", for they won't satisfy the cravings. You know when you have a true appetite for revival when you seemingly become obsessed with all things God. Beyond a church meeting and service, you become hungry and start to crave for the things of God like you've never craved. You try to find it in conferences, books, church trends, and all of the sorts. There's a longing for something else.

You wake up in the middle of the night and listen to worship music, you find yourself pacing the floor humming and singing little songs, praying, and reading the bible.

TRUE REVIVAL is birthed in the agonizing of the soul for something more than what you have. You want more than fun church and a preacher with a hipster message, you want the power of God. The stirring of the soul causes you to quest after the unknown. We may not know all we're reaching for at first, may not even know what we're after, but revival brings a yearning that can't be tamed with any substitutes.

Every believer ought to desire to be stirred. Revival is built on the back of people whose souls were stirred, passions were pure, and hearts ablaze.

Ask God to sanctify your appetite. Examine

yourself. Take an introspective look within, and allow God to cleanse you of the things you crave. Without a stirring, you'll go from trend to trend seeking after what you can not see. Don't accept and do not settle. There is more.

No man practices HIS presence accept He stirs them to.

PRAYER.

Once you receive a burden for the presence of God you must pray it through. I'll deal with this in great emphasis in the next section, however, prayer is the key to revival.

Prayer teams are essential to moves of God. I strongly recommend various types of individuals with no agenda. I personally think teams of people from various churches, reformations, and assemblies are even better. It helps to keep the chatter and gossip down when we're not gathered to talk about one another, and to make unofficial church councils and pastors aide committees. When we gather from various places, we can keep the main the thing, the main thing.

Assemble your core team. Maybe you'll pray together every Tuesday or perhaps every Friday. Agree on a time, place, and burden. Unify yourselves through intercession. Build a strong and strategic team by emphasizing the need for corporate momentum. Find one person that wants to see God the way you desire to see Him and start from there.

I often tell people to imagine what would happen if instead of 100 people coming to complain about their disinterests in the church, they came and prayed for deliverance, healing, a nd change within. PRAY for guidance, answers, and solutions. Intercessors don't murmur about the world, they change it! Use the eyes you have to see beyond the flaws and see the possibility of an amazing recovery.

Ask God to show you how to pray. Allow the spirit to pray through you. Don't allow yourself to pray your pity or your emotions, but pray the will of God. For it is true that we know not how to pray as we should, but the Spirit itself makes intercession with moans and groans that can't be uttered (Romans 8:26).

Pray as the SPIRIT leads.

F E L L O W S H I P.

You will NEVER see true revival alone. No single man or woman can say, that a major move of God was started because of their prayers or faith solely. "God used me to do it" is never on the lips of a true revivalist. It's a team effort. God meant us to do this together.

We must first have fellowship with HOLY SPIRIT. Talk to Him. Sing with/to HIM. The person of the Holy Spirit is as real as the person you walk pass down the street. He's real. Fellowship with HIM keeps you ahead of the game.

Not only is fellowship with HOLY SPIRIT essential, but you must have fellowship with one another.

There is beauty in being able to connect with likeminded people that share your heart and passion for Jesus. There's a strength that comes when believers band together as one.

The one thing that Babel, Jericho, and Jerusalem all had in common were people with one mind. The heavens take great pleasure in unity. It's like precious oil that flowed from the beard of Aaron. The bible says that when believers dwell in unity…it's good (Ps. 133:1)! Contention, drama, and envy should be named among unbelievers. Believers dwell in harmony because heaven is in harmony.

We read no where in scripture where angels fight who will get to sing Amen and who will get to sing Holy. They don't fight over notes or pitch. They sing aloud with one voice *Holy! Holy! Holy!* Those creatures around the throne worship in such harmony until it shakes the heavens and rattles the earth. There's power in a unified body. We can do more damage to the powers of hell singing the same song than we can ever trying to be individual wonders.

Connect. Get to know the hearts of those that are around you. Build through relationship. Bare each other's burdens and then lift each other up in prayer. REVIVAL is costly, and some give up along the way. Be discerning and be compassionate. Have the heart of God that sees past the weakness and the frailty of others, and pick them up in the spirit of intercession until they're back on track.

Share revelations, exchange burdens. Imagine spending hours talking about the scripture instead of about each other. Become one body.

PURITY.

CONSECRATION is the science of maturity. You can't be like HIM and be like you at the same time. Holy times calls for holy people. And I know that God can use anyone. I know that grace is available and that we were once all in sin and blah blah, blah blah, blah blah, and everything else people tend to message me about in rebuttal to the things I write and speak on. I get all of that, and most of it, I agree with.

At the end of the day, you can't pursue revival with dirty hands. For even as much as David loved God, and God loved David, he was disqualified for building God a house because of bloody hands (I Chronicles 28:3). God looks for men/women with clean hands and a pure heart that will pursue Him in the right spirit.

If you're after "revival" because you think it's going to "put you on"—this isn't for you. If your motive is to preach the message of revival because it sounds good to you, all your friends are preaching it, you're seeing people write books about it, or that it seeming has become trendy…it's not for you to run with.

BUILDING REVIVAL IS FOR THE PURE IN HEART! The messengers of revival are those that have no agenda but The Holy Spirit. If you're one that loves to be in charge or control…this isn't for you. Revival cancels your "bookings", it disrupts your programs, some days you don't get to preach, it inconveniences your plans back at home. True revival does what it wants. Remember it is the SPIRIT of RESSURECTION that fuels revival. Wherever the dead is found, there is the potential for revival. It's without time constraints and it can't be rushed. REVIVAL CULURE is only for those that desire to walk in purity.

CONTEND FOR IT

I read about William Seymour and how he kept his head in a box until it was time for the Lord to speak. I remember reading once about how Frank Bartleman, one of the figureheads during the 1900 outpouring, was so desperate to see God, that he would fast and go without food until his wife became worried and nervous of his heath. One day, Bro. Bartleman and his friend were speaking, and the power of God sat upon them both so heavy, that he began to cry and travail until the point to where he wrote it felt as if he was in physical pain. He contended for an outpouring.

He reached a place of desperation, that all he

wanted was God. He didn't care about food, he didn't care about man, he didn't care about anything other than seeing Holy Spirit.

Here's how you contend for revival:

- Don't Relent. Don't give up. Pray and keep praying. Cry and keep crying. Don't run from the burden because it seems like a lost cause. Don't quit because it seems as if the trend has died down. Pursue and give it all you have. Time has a way of vetting out the inconsistent and those that aren't serious. When the trend dies, you'll notice some will go right along with it.

I've seen all sorts of trends and movements in my short time alive on the earth. I've seen obsessions with anointing oils, handkerchiefs, prayer clothes, prayer shawls, all sorts of things. I've seen sacred things over sensationalized to the point to where we no longer see the true biblical perspective of them anymore.

In the years of church trends, I've seen us make worship and prayer "movements" something cool when it's essential to Christian living. I've seen people "taught" and "coached on how to speak in tongues and given the proper phrases to say in order to sound gifted and get somewhere within the body. But all in all, when the trends died, I witnessed people jump ship.

Those that have a burden will never jump ship. It's been over ten years, and I still see the same glory that visited me in my sleep. I still sense the same power that I would cry and lock myself away in a room for days at a time. There is a burden to see dead men come back to life that no matter what trend I try to follow, I'll never lose my pursuit.

Don't let church trends make you lose your burden!

- War For Regions. Bad territories and areas that seem *"unpopular for building"* are prayer targets. Dry land and dead bones aren't always a sign that you should be running from there, some times, it's the very *confirmation* you keep seeking and answer that you're really suppose to be there.

Just as there are principalities and certain spirits that reside over regions and areas, someone has to take up the hedge and begin to pray the will of God into drug infested areas. Who will take prayer walks around our schools and cry out to God for the end of gun-violence, suicide, and bullying that goes on within our schools today?

REVIVALS are very much intentional. The Spirit of the Lord is upon, for He has anointed me to________. GLORY comes with assignment. What is the burden of your hunger? What pricks your heart?

Will you commit yourself to war and contend for people, struggles, and nations until you see breakthrough, deliverance, and true encounters with God?

On the flip side of that, another thing about regions and revivals is knowing where you're called to be. It pays to have communion with Holy Spirit. You see, it all ties in. You can be in a region or working on something for years seeing little to no results, and it may not be that it's "not your time" it may be that you're in the wrong region. You may just be out of place.

Proper placement breeds proper pour. He pours out in areas where both heaven and earth agree.

chapter three

BURNING FIELDS.

Then Jesus went about all the cities and villages, teaching in their synagogues, preaching the gospel of the kingdom, and healing every sickness and every disease among the people. But when He saw the multitudes, He was moved with compassion for them, because they were weary and scattered, like sheep having no shepherd. Then He said to His disciples, "The harvest truly *is* plentiful, but the laborers *are* few. Therefore pray the Lord of the harvest to send out laborers into His harvest."

-Matthew 9:35-38

W E NEED A PREACHER. There is a field ripe and ready for REVIVAL. There is a valley of dead men's bones ready to live again. As evil, grim, and wicked as you may see the world, it's nothing more than a field! The harvest seems to be expanding. I'm going to go out on a limb here, and express my opinions. As sin grows, the field widens. It's growing and gaining ground. But much like Jesus, I must admit, I'm a bit disheartened.

Every few years there is an influx of certain gifts and offices within our culture of "church"—especially among charismatics. Coming up, everyone wanted to be an "Evangelist" but not the real kind. We went from that, to prophets and prophetesses —everyone wanted to be prophetic and carry the governmental office of such. We went from that phase to the Bishop. So many bishops, so little responsibilities. And now Bishops are competing and at war with the apostles. ***I'm more anointed, no, I'm more anointed.*** " Bishops are fighting to become apostles, and apostles are changing to become bishops and we're going back and forth because we can't seem to figure out who is "in charge."

There is a mass exodus taking place in the course of our antics and political explorations. People are dying. Our churches are seemingly becoming fuller and emptier at the same time. We're swapping dead men's bones, and it seems as though (not as a whole), but no one cares. Where are the preachers? Where are the (wo)men who go into the fields and go fishing for the souls? Who has the burden for souls?

Once upon a time, churches and ministries would hit the block, and they would walk up and down the streets, passing out pamphlets, knock on doors, and invite people to come out to the church. People would invite their co-workers, they would tell their friends and families about the church. It seems as if our modern conveniences have made many including myself lazy in our evangelistic responsibilities. It takes more than a Facebook tag in your churches flyer to evangelize. We. NEED. A. PREACHER.

THE INTERCESSOR.

> I looked for someone to stand up for me against all this, to repair the defenses of the city, to take a stand for me and stand in the gap to protect this land so I wouldn't have to destroy it. I couldn't find anyone.
>
> -Ezekiel 22:30 (MSG)

At the helm of every great move of the spirit, there are people who are called simply to pray. Not to beat a dead horse or to re-write what has been written in an earlier chapter, but God looks for someone to war in the spirit. He looks for a man or a woman that will pray great restoration into regions. He looks for someone to take up the hedge and to stop those princes, forces, and powers through prayer and intercession.

He looks for people that go out into the streets of a crime-infested city, and declare that the city belongs to

God. What pleases God is the heart of a man that will meet Him every day and war for the economics in their city. He looks for a man/woman to stand in the gap for a burden, and stick it out until they see change.

There are countless millions saved and serving the Lord now, because someone prayed for them. God has used women who couldn't even preach, to pray many of the great men of God we have come to know through dark nights and seasons.

God looks for men/women that will cry for a burden. Ask God for something bigger than you. Pray for passion. Pray for something beyond, "bless me". I've been more moved to pray that the Lord gives me a heart to be moved with compassion much like HIS. I want to be burdened by the things that make HIM weep. I want to know what makes HIM smile. I want to know the joy in seeing people free that HE experiences. I want to know the type of joy that causes HIM to dance over us. I want a burden for souls.

He looks for men/women that HE can trust with a burden. Can God depend on you to get the job done? It's not enough to pray when you feel like it, but can HE trust you with taking up the hedge? Will you get up in the middle of the night? Will you stop eating, break your plans, go and seek God for a week without any explanation and without blasting it for people to know and see?

Intercessors have trust with God. He has to be able to trust you with pressure. Can He trust you with secrets and battle plans? It's impossible to be loosed-mouth and be an intercessor. You can't prey on me and pray for me at the same time. Intercessors must have discipline, and see no self-gain as a result of their intercession. Intercessors are not gossipers. You can't tell someone that you're praying for them, have them confide in you, and share their business over dinnertime. It's unethical, not integral, and not in good character.

THE EVANGELIST.

As a kid, I thought ministry went by "ranking" and from office to office depending on your tenure and such. From what I often seen and noticed around me, first you were a deacon, then if you were a man or a "boring" preacher, you became a minister, then you went to an elder. In my mind, after that, you became a pastor, and from a pastor an overseer, and then a bishop. I saw so many succeed through such and thought that was how it worked.

Apostles, prophets, and evangelists were three gifts that were always in the "other" category for me. The apostle and prophet—they were nearly extinct; however in the 90's, I started to see them in title more and more. The ministry of the evangelist was one that was very unique because as a kid, though it wasn't taught, I always thought that gift was reserved for women because they were the only ones I seen.

They were typically fiery and prophetic. Services were usually on youth nights, "revival" meetings, and generally would be gathered crowds from various churches. Their messages were generally convicting and sharp, and their altar calls were DYNAMIC. In some circles, Evangelist were given as titles to the women and that was it. They couldn't pastor, or be in top tiers of ministry/leadership…but somehow, once being "accepted" into the ranks of ministry, "Evangelist" was a title that I seen slapped on many of them. For years, I had a very wrong view and perception of the gift. Even with my studying, my understanding was a bit jaded. In my mind, someone was wrong. Either a great deal of the evangelists that I came to know were not real evangelists, or what I was learning and studying about was outdated…either way, I had questions.

Coming into 2018, the Lord really began to speak heavily about The EVAGELIST to me. I mean, it was in great detail and with such an urgency. I started to consult HIM as if I was operating in the right gift, because The EVANGELIST seemed to be where the goods were at. He spoke and said, "My eyes are upon the evangelist." He kept speaking it over and over again.

I began to reach out to those in the five fold community—elders and wise counsel within the church, about what God had been dealing with me about, and to my comfort, many of them had been experiencing the same urgings of the Lord.

REVIVAL is fueled by the heart of people that will declare HIS wonders masterfully among a dark and grim world. EVANGELISTS are light bearers. They invade dark spaces and stir the hearts, souls, and faiths of the dead and dying.

There are too many dead men in dead cities for us to fight over church rows and recognition. We keep trying to build and become the biggest church and the most powerful church, and the Lord is simply asking, "who shall I send?". Who will lay their position down and hit the field running? Who shall take up the burden for the dead? Dead men can't travel. Do you remember the story of the demoniac that was there in the Gadarenes? The man was tied up, lived in cemeteries among tombs and graves. He was often bound with chains and fetters because of his oppression (see Luke 8:26-39).

I know modern church has made "sin" cute and we've been desensitized to the affects of bondage, but there are some real oppressed people out there. HELL is REAL. SATAN is REAL. There are some people that are tied up, bound, and shackled. They will never come into your tent meeting. They'll never wander into your church. These oppressed people will never step foot in your convocation—but they will encounter you. Will you go for GOD, in the name of God, with the power of God to break the spells and bands of wickedness?

There is a real tangible and weighty glory available and accessible for those willing to go for God. There is a harvest of dead bones. The RESSURECTION desires partnership. Ezekiel came into agreement with HIM. EVANGELISTS work with urgency to see the dying and dead made alive again through the word and demonstration of JESUS.

It is impossible to be an evangelist and don't know the bible. All demons are not foolish. There are some highly intelligent spirits—principalities with ancient knowledge and world wisdom. They'll argue your bible with your bible and leave you bewildered. You must know THE WORD. Study. Make time to grow in your faith. Know what you believe and why you believe it. Be well versed, sharp, and ready. Become so full of the WORD that it bubbles over and out of you.

The evangelist must be compassionate. You can't love GOD and hate people. Evangelists can't hate "faggots" and spew hate in the name of God. Anyone called to this way of life, can be seen with the whoremonger and be unshaken. They're not easily offended by the drinker's smell, or the prostitutes' attire…they see the soul. The message of a sent one must be that which talks about the LOVE of God so much that

He made a way of escape. FEAR is not the source of the message. That stuff is cute inside the confines of the church, but it doesn't work on unbelievers. You can't scare them into salvation.

The evangelist of our day must tell the story. Be quick and instant, preach each sermon as if you have just a few moments to snatch someone's soul out of hell. THERE IS AN URGENCY. Ask God to give you a burden and to feel the weight of your disobedience. Ask Him to allow you to see the people who will die in the valley because you refuse to go.

WE NEED A FISHERMEN.

All of these church people and churches can't keep needing reviving. WHY do we keep dying so fast? What's the problem? Someone has to leave the church with that power and go DEMONSTRATE God in dead places.

The REVIVALIST

There is coming a wave of men/women that will move not just with great articulation and intelligence, but in DEMENSTRATION. There is no value in our words if we have no power to prove it.

I remember as a kid making bold claims, or my friends saying things, and when you didn't believe someone, you said, "prove it" –because you knew in all confidence that they were full of bluff or that they couldn't make a sufficient case. Every so often, you'd encounter that kid that wasn't impressed with your story, your facts, and creative story telling just didn't work. They wanted to see the proof. If you lied and said you had money, they wanted to see. If you said you could do more backflips than them, they wanted to see. You couldn't weasel your way out by making up an excuse. You had to "put up or shut up" as it's coined.

This is the hour where you must PROVE your Jesus in wonders! God raises up revivalist to set cities ablaze. They're not interested in starting organizations, denominations, reformations, and gaining cliques and crews. Their focus is LIFE.

God has groomed these men and women to stand alone but with a force of many. Often revivalist are singled out from local churches and communities and tend to meet up with other revivalists by divine connections, supernatural moments, and by way of the Spirit. Covenant relationships are key to revivalists. They're not so easy to be "friends" with just everyone. They value those in their life and they have fruit from those connections.

REVIVALISTS walk in a blaze of fire, they're always ready to rise to the occasion. They're men and women of passion. It's not a job, it's not a task, it's not a great burden. They WANT to see people whole. It's their passion to see the dead come alive again. They look for moments to be used by God without recognition. They cast out devils in malls. They lay hands on the sick in back halls. They don't wait to be invited or go around passing out "book me" cards/flyers. Wherever they go—fire follows them.

REVIVAL power looks like the bones of Elisha waking up the dead man whose bones touched his (II Kings 13:21). It resembles the shadow of Peter that healed the sick and impotent that laid in the street on mats and beds (Acts 5:15-16). Jesus was revival. Remember when He showed up into the Gergesenes and was met with two men possessed by evil spirits? They screamed, "why have you come to torment us before our time?" (Matthew 8:28). REVIVALIST unnerve principalities. Without announcement, they interrupt regions.

People of revival, contend with religious principalities. They upset systems. Samuel in the courts of Eli confronted a corrupt system. There are those that have been marked to deal with and to confront religious spirits that bind and stop-up the river of God from flowing. This new breed of revivalist are plugged in, to what heaven has to say and aren't afraid of losing popularity or friendship. They're fueled by righteousness, and motivated by love.

The tides are shifting. The coasts are changing. God has an army that will destroy the works of the devil. We will not be shaken. HEAVEN has a witness, and earth has a prophet. Make way for the voice of the preacher!

chapter four
POWER!

I love the supernatural. My late mentor, David Huskins often said that the supernatural is more real than the world around us. There are moments I find myself attempting to contain this spiritual high I tend to find myself in. I'll sit in and gaze into the presence of the Lord at times for hours, and that can become overwhelming. I took the word of God to heart where it commanded that we should, "walk in the Spirit" (Galatians 5:16). I don't believe that the Spirit world was meant for church and church days. I believe now and have always believed that if you're going to be a man on fire for God, then you were suppose to constantly stay lit. The flames are to always be alive. Practicing HIS presence on a daily basis keeps the heart and spirit from waxing cold. I believe that the keys to accessing greater dimensions and realms of God's power is simply intimacy and faith.

Some years ago I found myself in a season of unusual visitations. I once would be hesitant and fearful to share such things out of risk of being mocked and not being accepted, however—I'm already where I want to be. I cannot be shaken. I find that when sharing, I'm amazed with others that can identify but have no one else to share with—or those that desire such encounters, I find such stories to stir the faith. *But I digress.*

Some days I felt as if I would leave my earthly body because of the weight that came from being in HIS presence. I didn't seek HIM for fame, or an opportunity to speak on platforms. I had a hunger and thirst after HIS righteousness, and I was determined to see HIM. If this JESUS of the bible was real, I wanted to meet HIM in a real way. I wanted to touch HIM, I wanted to feel and walk in HIS power. I wanted to see what heaven saw. I wanted to hear the sounds of HIS intercession for me. My quest and desire led me on wild journeys in HIM and led by HIM.

I believe wholeheartedly that we are embarking upon an age where the supernatural will become more common than uncommon. It already has, actually. Look at our world around us. The earth is consumed with mediums, spiritualists, and people intrigued with the other side. Culture has an obsession with the supernatural. Our world is engulfed. From cartoons and blockbuster films, we're constantly inundated with a one sided, misguided, and demonic angle of the supernatural. Where is the church? I believe this is something that the church should confront head-on. We must catch up to the age, and drink of the river and demonstrate HIM big in the earth or we will lose a generation.

Instead of picketing, rioting, and signing petitions to get shows off the air and events shut down—I think the intercessors and the watchmen need to rise up like Elijah, and engage in the showdown! God has marked some people to contend with the powers of this age by simply walking in authentic demonstration. You won't have to war and waste time telling everyone how bad or off the other stuff is. But when you show up in authentic power—the truth of who CHRIST is will yield results. Be not afraid to speak out. For this indeed is a great hour for the supernatural.

The ASCENSION: Come Away With Me.

Times and seasons of great encounters with HIM are on the horizon. There are some places in GOD and waters of the supernatural that even your favorite evangelists haven't even tapped. There's a place in God where the waters are deep and the winds are strong. Who will be daring to pursue after such a current? Great times with HIM awaits the willing.

I was at work one day, and the Lord filled my mouth with a song. I began to sing the Song of the Lord, and He spoke, "come away with Me my child, come away with Me my beloved. Come away with me my chosen one, and I will show you things, that you know not of." There are some things reserved for those that are willing to COME.

We have an invitation into the supernatural. We have entry into the heavens. God is looking to gather a HOLY NATION to bring them into a realm of demonstration for this hour. But this is not the type of power where you just stumble into it. This won't be transferred via your favorite preacher, and nobody will be able to confeer it to you. As much as I am an advocate for school, your degree can't get it for you. Having a pretty brand and being picture perfect won't get you access either.

This is a power and a weight that can only be given by The Spirit. We have access—the door of the Spirit is open, but whosoever will—let him come! You have to come up higher. Be willing to come as HE leads. Are you willing to go?

Who shall ascend into the hill of the Lord? Who shall be found in the courts and gates of our God? He's looking for a desperate soul that simply wants HIM. He has things to show you and things to tell you. May He cleanse our desire to know HIM even the more. May passion for CHRIST come alive and be quickened within us again!!

RIVER MUSIC.

Speaking to yourselves in psalms, hymns, and spiritual songs, making melodies in your heart to the Lord.
-Ephesians 5:19

And I heard a sound from heaven like the roar of rushing waters and the loud rumbling of thunder. And the sound I heard was like harpists strumming their harps. And they sang a new song before the throne and before the four living creatures and the elders. And no one could learn the song except the one hundred forty-four thousand who had been redeemed from the earth.

Revelations 14:2-3

One of the greatest distrusts of God's creativity in you is to steal the style of another. I understand what's trending maybe easy to mirror, and I'm not downplaying being influenced at all. But I believe there is in each of us an ability to create. There are sounds and songs uncharted and unheard. There are chants, praises, and cords going around the throne that we can't even imagine.

Words and languages that aren't even created are unlocked when one commits themself to spending time soaking in HIS presence. I believe He gives downloads straight from the RIVER to your spirit that comes second to none in originality and creativity. We're singing hymns and songs given decades ago, because someone took a sip from the river. There are people whose music got them tossed out of churches and were banned from choirs simply because it didn't sound like the current noise. God simply unleashed a new sound in the earth.

Be not afraid. Sing a new song! Work with the SPIRIT and go with the flow. Rivers flow, they don't skip and jump, and splash here and there. The streams are steady! Songs of the Spirit aren't forced and they aren't hard to master. The Spirit, Himself sings beautiful medleys over us, and through us. I was going through my iCloud and my recorded voice memos and clips, I realized I have over 30 hours of songs given by The Spirit. It's one of the strangest things about me I think. I'll began to sing in the Spirit and the melodies will accompany the songs. With no drummer, no pianist, I'll be given both words and cords to things from THE RIVER. While I'm not sure if I'll ever do anything with them, I do have them and listen to them periodically as strength to my own spiritual progression.

Around the throne of God there are degrees of songs and volumes of praise. Certain songs are reserved for a remnant chosen to carry that sound. RIVER MUSIC is LIFE MUSIC. They sing about the present, they sing about the future. What a wonder, that HEAVEN can sing over us in the most melodious way. In the river there are SONGS of WAR—there is no defeat in them. They are songs of the ultimate DELIVERANCE. They praise God for winning the fights we in ourselves would be defeated in. RIVER MUSIC are songs of prophecy. They tell you how the battle ends before it begins. You remember Miriam, the prophetess? The bible recalls one of my favorite stories in Exodus 15.

She picks up her timbrel and began to sing in response to Moses and the children of Israel of how the Lord had overthrown both the horse and his rider, and had given them the victory. We are moving into perilous times, and I believe that as the world grows dark, not only will He give us just songs to declare our love for HIM, but also songs of war. He is changing the way we fight and do battle. No longer will we be intimated and sit in corners crying or begging that our situations change. But I believe in the RIVER is a new battle song. You'll fight but you'll win. New chants and sounds of victory are being downloaded for this age.

Sing a NEW song! There is something supernatural about a fresh melody. Make melodies within your heart. Sing ALOUD. Let your voice be heard! Let the nations know that The LORD is GOD!

In the coming days, "worship" will no longer be stagnant and simply entertainment. We will not gather to simply see what notes our worship teams sing, if they're singing our favorite songs, or any of that. It will no longer be something we do until the preacher comes. As we taste of the age to come, God is changing the perspective, passion, and design of worship in many of our western churches. I believe that a purity is coming to the center of our music. There will be less about us and our needs and more on HIM and HIS righteousness. I believe in order, but I believe there is coming a moment in time where worship leaders and departments are going to began to go off the grid. You won't be able to follow them on a big screen. They'll start with one song and sing it for 20 minutes and soak in the presence of the Lord.

I believe He's sending a fresh wave to the sound of the church. Musicians won't be looked at as property or just seen as "help." We will see them as prophetic components used to usher in waves. The days where orgies and seeing music as nothing more than another "gig", no different from the club have ended. There's a sacredness that's coming to the arts. I believe that God is raising up skilled men (and women). For years we felt like it had to be one or the other. Growing up in my culture of Pentecost, we (not my home church in particular) were so anxious to have music in the church, that we let anyone play. Can't read music? That's okay. You only know two keys? That's fine. We had no standard and we were content with the bare minimum. But no longer will that be the norm.

Skill musicians with both ability and anointing will be the standard. God is going to prick the hearts of those who receive to ensure that his anointed are taken care of with integrity also. No longer will we mishandle those that render their gifts to God. God is concerned about it all.

Your musicians will prophesy. Your praise team will prophesy. You church will prophesy. Sing songs together. Worship is EVERYONES responsibility. They may have the microphone, but it is the job of us all to engage the moment. I'm not too sure what it's called now, but as a kid, we called the music in the beginning of church, "devotion", then we called it praise and worship. Devotions were usually done when the "singers" of the church weren't really there. It was usually just a few people with a tune, that could carry a note. They would sing "congregational songs" and hymns. They had "testimony" time, where they would let a few people get up and give a tale of thanksgiving. They would get up and say, "First giving honor to God who is the head of my life. I thank God for being saved, sanctified, filled with the Holy Ghost and that with a mighty burning fire. To the pastor, members, and visitors…I thank God…" and would go on with their story until they got carried away and had to get the microphone taken back and another song would start.

It was a time in God that often took a while to pass. Some times it was done waiting for the preacher or the rest of the church to show up. Then we progressed to "praise and worship." It was different from the choir. These were just a handful of people that would pump us and get us ready for church. I used to watch many use this time to fellowship, arrive, and do all sorts of thing but engage in the moment. Pastors and preachers would stay in the back office, and sit and gossip, and do all sorts of "doc" things while the people are in the temple.

I've watched this portion of service so mishandled. We think Praise and Worship is just singing songs. To label praise as a fast song and worship as a slow song is to completely miss what God is attempting to do in your faith community at that moment. He wants melodies from your heart. He wants a song from you. We ought not sit needing to be entertained, but we must engage in the very moment.

God wants to BRING BACK THE SOUND, unscripted and unparalleled. During the Azusa Street REVIVAL, it's reported that at times as led by Bro. Seymour, they would began to sing in the Spirit, and it would almost become as if they were in heaven. They had no one to fix their microphones, they had no script of what to sing next, they sung according to HIS leading. They sang and heard sounds not of this earth. They had no one to fix their microphones, they had no script of what to sing next, they sung according to HIS leading. I remember days watching the Brownsville Outpouring play out as a kid. There would be times of intense soaking where a song would start and they would just sit weeping and crying out to God for a while before a preacher dared to step to the podium and touch a microphone.

When I moved to Pennsylvania some years ago, the Lord sent me to a church that would follow the spirit in such a way, that some services for a season we never made it past worship. The spirit would fall so until there was no offering, no one spent time looking at their phones or watches. We flowed with the RIVER until people were transformed in the presence of the Lord, and would return in the middle of the week for bible study to grow and learn about what they were experiencing on Sunday mornings. The GLORY was among us. We didn't have a sound system. In fact in our early days, we started out in a house, and we would encounter HIM weekly.

I'm not saying abandon your playlist, what I am saying is follow HIM. You can't create a glory that you don't live in. Make time to host Holy Spirit. Sing with HIM, allow God to become the center of your life's song. Ministry moments are changing drastically, and the only way you're going to be able to keep up or advance pass the culture is to be drenched in the Holy Spirit and be not afraid to be different.

SING!

chapter five
MAINIFESTING WONDERS

Growing up, there were two things I always knew; I knew the presence of Holy Spirit and I knew that He gave the church power to heal the sick. Throughout my childhood, I didn't even know what the prophetic or a prophet was. I thought everyone talked to God like this. I thought everyone was having these "weird" moments like me. I knew God before I knew that I knew Him. I would seek after ministries, aspire to be like people, and desire to hear God or have relationship with HIM, all the while, I had it all along. So that, I can't really describe, I can't tell you how I knew other than the fact that I just knew. While I never shared it, as I grew, people would give words of knowledge and speak and confirm it.

The other thing I knew as a kid was that I was going to manifest wonders. Before I knew what a bishop was, before I knew the function of a prophet, before I knew about branding and even all the books of the bible, I knew that I was going to see sick people healed, I knew that I would see the oppressed free, and I knew that I would see dead men raised to life again. It was my conviction, it was my passion, and it was my song. I wanted God to use me to bring moves of God into the earth. Now, while, as I've gotten older, so has my perspective on "glory"—but I knew as a kid, what I desired to do. I didn't know if I would be picked to carry such a task, but it was my passion to pursue in hopes that if He needed me, I would be available without limitations.

As I got older, I found myself enamored with the supernatural and the word of God. The stories where HE spoke fascinated me. To examine the life of the prophets, and my favorite—the construction of the tabernacle would leave me memorized for months. I would study books for months at a time, without ever reading any other books hardly, simply out of fascination of how HE would choose to reveal Himself. I grew in that. And I must admit, though, I've progressed, I'm a far better Old Testament story teller than new. I can break down Exodus faster than I can type in my password for most of my logins.

My study habits were weird and off, and so was my prayer time and worship. I found myself as mentioned in earlier chapters chanting and singing a lot. I would sing songs in the spirit and I would do all sorts of things that weren't really normal in my mind.

When I began preaching, I found myself trying to be like the idea of what successful ministry looked like in hopes of being "picked". I preached like my favorite thinkers and speakers and that would flop. I went through the phrase of trying to fit into the crew with all the boy preachers and that didn't work. I remember not having a collar or being able to afford one as a kid, so I would wear a black shirt and white collar and black tie, and I would go to the corner store to get a fake gold chain to put in my pocket, to attempt to look like what I thought was a preacher.

I went through many stages attempting to find myself. I went through a hollering phase where I thought I had to yell to prophesy. I even went through deep talking and using super long words that I didn't understand to convey my point. Any and everything you can think of to try to "find my way"—I did. While I have some sort of training, people often ask about my hermeneutical approach to the scriptures, and I tell them, it came from being a boy with too much time on his hands. I would sit and read the scriptures, type sermons, and record myself on my cassette player that could record. Then I moved to mp3 player. I would write sermons day and nights, and preach to myself. And I would tell myself, "when I preach one day". Usually a once a year youth service…this is how I'm going to do it.

I did all of that and went through that whole phase. And then one day, as I matured, found myself becoming less and less impressed and more content with being who God made me to be. When I learned who I was, it was okay to be me without fear and without hassle. I grew in God and began to allow God to led my life.

As a kid, I had a fiery passion and burden to host an event where GOD would be GOD. I wanted people to fall in love again with the power of God without the rules and regulations of "church moments." My childhood mentor Carlton Pearson told me many years ago, "God is looking for just ONE person, ONE conference and ONE man that will let HIM have HIS way—when He finds that ONE it will be unstoppable." I wanted to be the one that gave God room to do whatever HE desired.

Ten years in ministry, I hosted my first conference. Full of fear, full of faith, and full of questions, I began to do what I had in my heart to do. It went completely left. Nothing went the way "I planned." While the Spirit of God was present, to me, it wasn't what I desired. In my mind, it would be packed, and full of awesome reviews, etc. I vowed that it wouldn't be like that again, and so the next year, attempted it, and changed things, and again—it turned out nothing like I planned. And I couldn't understand why. I was hurt, crushed, and embarrassed.

It was confusing to me because I KNEW without a shadow of doubt that GOD gave it and released me to do it, yet things just wasn't coming together. I had friends and people close to me watch things play out with that and just with ministry in general. They were all over the place preaching and quite poplar for their regions and in their spheres be it singer and or preacher. I sat with a group of some of my close friends one day, and they said, "the reason what you're trying to do isn't working is because you're not brandable. You're weird and your delivery will never get you anywhere". Another chimed in and said, "you're not big enough to do what you're trying to do". That crushed me. I could handle being told that I needed to change the packaging or things about how I was going about what I was attempting to build, but to be told that what I have didn't work—it wounded me a little.

I started to reshape me and what I had to mirror brands of successful young leaders. I would attempt to get up and get preaching clips that I could make appealing to draw a crowd. I was attempting to center the things I was doing around what was working for others. I felt like I was going in a circle. I was trying to preach, brand and do things like everyone and it still wasn't working. Still, no one was listening. Still, no one was watching. I'd just written a book that became an independent best seller from my distribution company, I had access to some of the most notable names in ministry, and yet nothing seemed to be moving. Periodically some prophetic voices would reach out to me and encourage the vision that I still had but now had "another way" of building it. I felt the leading of the Lord to come away, yet I fought it to attempt to build something that simply wasn't working.

One day, The Lord spoke to me and said, "you're building this thing without ME. NONE OF THIS is what I gave you. I didn't give you a blueprint, I gave you a RIVER." Immediately conviction hit me. I shut everything down, social media, ministering, every plan, every idea, I through it all on the altar. I had to repent. Reality is, I got so lost in trying to build for God, I neglected to stay in the RIVER. I got stuck and complacent. I found myself trying to be everything other than what I knew to be. I left my source. I went through a season where I stopped moving and simply allowed things to just "exist". Nothing was happening, and nothing was going on. I was doing things, simply so that I could tell people, I was doing something. Trying to keep up with the latest flyers and keep up with the latest conferences and trends will dry you up quickly.

During my time where I came away, my desire came alive again. I abandoned all I knew and thought I knew and cried for GOD afresh again. There has to be more than this. There has to be more than just being a preacher. I want to be more than just a guy on a flyer. I don't want to preach, I don't want to write, I don't want to exist just to be here. There is a RIVER in my belly and the waters must flow. RIVERS move. There is a flow. To be stuck or stagnant is an indication that there are problems in the stream.

I told God to strip it away. I had to remember the song I had before I had a platform. Some seasons of isolation isn't a matter of "sin" but a matter of heart. When you LOVE HIM, you can't exist outside of a healthy relationship with HIM. Have you ever been in love? Do you know what it's like to do things and have a career and build a life outside of the one you're with? God was my source. He was my "plug"—He was my brand. I had to bring it all back down and bring it back to nothing. Everything I thought I was, I had to bring low, everything I was attempting to build, I sacrificed at the altar. I desired my river back.

Ministry without a flow is bad religion. Prayer without a flow is a boring conversation. A life without a flow is an untapped existence. RIVERS FLOW. We need movement. We need a flow. We need people that will abandon all that they are, and repent for trying to do it their own way. Building without God will result in humiliating defeats. You can't build without HIM.

GO GET THE ARK

After I humbled and repositioned myself, I found myself in a season of GLORY. No invitations to preach, and no visible name—I was in the place that I started. I was in the middle of the river. The Lord spoke and said, "now that you're back at the center, go back to the initial instruction: Go GET THE ARK!" Immediately, it stirred me. It was as if I was ignited once again.

Throughout the next few weeks, the Lord would speak with such an urgency and authority:

GO GET THE ARK!

GO GET THE ARK!

GO GET THE ARK!

This was indeed a mandate from God. My mind flooded with messages, concepts, events, and things to do. And I said to myself, "chill—let's see where He wants to take this". I've studied the tabernacle for years and thought maybe a book on the Shekinah Glory, or maybe a conference about the Ark of The Covenant. I wasn't sure exactly what He meant, and He began to fill me in along the way. Holy Spirit gave me a few keys to understanding this mandate.

CAPTURED.

Then a man of Benjamin ran from the battle line the same day, and came to Shiloh with his clothes torn and dirt on his head. Now when he came, there was Eli, sitting on a seat by the wayside watching, for his heart trembled for the ark of God. And when the man came into the city and told it, all the city cried out. When Eli heard the noise of the outcry, he said, "What does the sound of this tumult mean?" And the man came quickly and told Eli. Eli was ninety-eight years old, and his eyes were so dim that he could not see. Then the man said to Eli, "I am he who came from the battle. And I fled today from the battle line." And he said, "What happened, my son?" So the messenger answered and said, "Israel has fled before the Philistines, and there has been a great slaughter among the people. Also your two sons, Hophni and Phinehas, are dead; and the ark of God has been captured." Then it happened, when he made mention of the ark of God, that Eli fell off the seat backward by the side of the gate; and his neck was broken and he died, for the man was old and heavy. And he had judged Israel forty years.

I Samuel 4:12- 18

Over the years, Holy Spirit has spoken some things to me, and have opened my eyes to some realities within our culture, church and earth. Most of what He's shared, I don't think I'll ever share. I don't believe He gives visions, dreams, and words all for you to blast and tell everyone. I believe that there should be a sacredness to secret baring with God. I believe that He reveals for a reason, and with that reason in mind, talking isn't always the point—being in place as a watchmen and burden-bearer is more ideal.

He took me on a journey in the supernatural some years ago, and He began showing me the state of the church. He began speaking things concerning what we consider "church" and much of the activities that surround us gathering, having local assemblies, etc. Before I start, let me just say, I LOVE the church. I know it's popular to bash the church and to talk about what's wrong with the church, however, I think it's vital to understand you can't love Christ and hate His Bride. I believe that the church STILL is alive, highly influential, and the purpose of the church is still valid. With that being said, I do wish to shine light on a few things that the Lord began to express over the years concerning The CHURCH.

I feel like Samuel at times in my ministry. My earliest memories of childhood were in church, my games as a kid, for the most part, centered around church. I dressed up in a sheet and preached to anyone that would listen to a child, even to toys and my sister's dolls—I was a church boy! I know what it's like to be in church all day and want to leave, and I know what it's like to be in church and can't leave. I've been in services where people were there until 1 and 2 in the morning because the power and presence of God prevailed and ruled the service. I remember convocation time when the saints would gather and seeing the most harmonic blend of gifts and expressions of Christ. I love the church, and while I know we advance and progress—this ain't what I grew to love.

Some days I sit frustrated not even wanting to attend church gatherings because it's all the same. We gather in the name of a personality or some sort of routine, we routinely dance and make sure we do it long enough so that we can edit and upload the clip of us dancing post service, we do all of these church things. We sing wonderfully, we preach articulately—we walk over chairs, we have pretty lights, and the packaging of JESUS is wonderful, but there is a fake in our midst.

I wholeheartedly believe that while we were trying to get in backrooms, on platforms, and in cahoots with the "in-crowd"—we possibly allowed tainted men to steal the ark! There is a generation that seen the glory, there's another that heard about the glory, and there is now a crowd that's creating their own glory based on what they've heard. We've made "glory" smoke/smog machines, big screens, and pretty lights. Our music is top notch and production is second to none, but God has never made it to many of our services.

Where is the RIVER? Where is The Glory? Where are those that come bearing His presence that's so thick that clouds began to form in the midst of their worship? We are building God's church with intelligence and entertainment, but there is no anointing. It's the anointing that breaks the yoke. It's the anointing of Christ that draws men and transforms.

There's a falling away and men's hearts are failing. There is a sound in the earth. There is a wail and a lamentation in the earth, because earth knows that the Glory has been captured. Our prayers aren't the same, our music isn't the same. Our priest aren't the same. Our lives aren't the same. There is something missing from the throne of our heart. It's HIS presence.

Israel began to shout because the ark of God was in their midst, and the Philistines heard them and said amongst themselves that they should go up and get the ark from them because they knew as a result of their sound, God was in their midst. Be not deceived, there are people who will never step foot in your church, but can recognized the power of a RESSURECTED CHRIST in your midst. Unbelievers no longer respect us because we've become too much like them. There is no distinction is our walk and in our sound. We sleep with them, we drink with them, we commit the profane with them, and then we attempt to minister to them in times of war—it doesn't work like that.

I've preached bound and have seen (by grace) people delivered. I've preached whole and have seen people free. Don't fool yourself by the agent called Grace. I don't want to be someone that walks in the shadows of grace. I don't want to be preaching with no glory. I don't want to pray for people and they remain the same. I want the glory!

ILLEGAL DWELLINGS.

Then the Philistines took the ark of God and brought it from Ebenezer to Ashdod. [2] When the Philistines took the ark of God, they brought it into the house of Dagon and set it by Dagon. [3] And when the people of Ashdod arose early in the morning, there was Dagon, fallen on its face to the earth before the Ark of The Lord. So they took Dagon and set it in its place again. [4] And when they arose early the next morning, there was Dagon, fallen on its face to the ground before the ark of the Lord. The head of Dagon and both the palms of its hands *were* broken off on the threshold; only Dagon's *torso* was left of it.

-I Samuel 5: 1- 5

We can only fake it for so long. When I began to write, I wanted to have the articulation that I had in previous writings. I wanted to have great biblical content that you could read for days, and I wanted to have footnotes galore full of books, research, and scholastic works that you could go and study at your leisure on the Glory and presence of God. But not really my speed in my emotions as I type. WE ARE IN TROUBLE. There is an urgency in the Spirit for those to walk in Resurrection Power, and God is in the coming days coming after those that are HIS.

There is a culture of people that God is grooming, and they are emerging as wrecking balls to the kingdom of hell. I declare that there are power gifts and supernatural anointings being groomed for the days to come that will dismantle ancient principalities and new age phenomenon.

There is a grace being disbursed even as I type, and God is making ready those that will bare HIS power without filter.

As the Lord exalts, we're going to see more and more models of success come down. We have tried to measure up to the first century church since we've left it. We've compared power and performance. We've reduced the supernatural to someone falling out that we've never seen fall out before. We've made ministry and church and we're trying to put them next to The Glory. You can't want glory and want to be famous at the same time. Your need for fame and popularity must be sacrificed if you're going to be one that carries REVIVAL.

The Lord said one day, "the Ole boys club is coming to an end." That old religious political regime where you have to play the game in order to be liked and accepted—God is bringing down. Superiority complexes, carnal backroom deals, and dirty conversations, they're all coming down. There is a purging by falling. And every fall doesn't have to be by "exposure". I think so many times we get so happy over public disgrace from leaders. No sir/no ma'am, I believe some will simply leave because of the overwhelming conviction that will happen within their hearts.

I believe with all my heart that God is going to judge religious systems that taught a generation how to have church without HIM. With our hyper-sensitive emotional messages, we've taught an entire generation how to pimp God and get away with it. We've stressed the importance of giving God our praise, dance, and money, but haven't stressed giving HIM our hearts. We've mastered "going in", yet haven't emphasized living IN THE SPIRIT. And we've done it all in the name of keeping a thriving crowd. Our systems are corrupt.

I believe the systems we've exalted above the kingdom, will be brought down low. As we see glory bearers arise, the need to be everyone's favorite will cease. This breed won't preach and raise offerings just to become a bishop. There won't be a need to go through the backdoor of ministry. He's sanctifying the temple!!

I saw the Lord bringing closure to the "pay-per-gift" movement. I won't have to pay in order to see you operate in the anointing. The value of what you have will supersede what I can give you. I believe one of the major things that is taking place in the new face of leadership, is that for many that are coming, they can't be bought. This prostitution ring has gone on long enough. He's pulling people from where they are and raising them up to show the world that you don't have to be poor to be anointed. I believe that God is going to fill the pockets and accounts of those whom He's calling, so that the world, worldly possessions, and things will not be the fall or snare that traps you. You will not be seduced by opportunities and won't be muzzled for a check.

Every place they took the ark, the bible said their idols would fall and that nothing worked. Some things are going to keep falling in our lives, until the ark is where it belongs. Your plans and God's plans are not equals. He has NO equal. His presence and power has NOTHING parallel to it. We can't keep trying to mirror something we don't have. HIS GLORY shouldn't belong on the shelf with every other common thing in your life.

We must return to having great reverence for the POWER of Almighty God and the supernatural. Men died mishandling HIS presence in days of old. There were those that God took the literal breath out of their body for placing His presence on a new cart. We are now in a new dispensation with grace, and don't have to fear that death to the same measure, but how much more should we live a life of holiness to HIM?

We've sat the glory in the backroom with the old hymnals, baptismal robes, and big bibles all in the name of "progression." We've progressed ourselves right into idolatry. We are the strength, the scent, and the source of our brand. And God has come to bring these things low through demonstration and through wonders. I see Babylon and the systems of this age falling.

GLORY is Coming! Altars are being repaired. Fresh flowing waters will flow once again from the sanctuaries of our God, and we must pursue after it!! Accept nothing less than GLORY. Stop being satisfied with cute church that looks like a rock concert, and bring back the ark!

Bring back the power, go get the anointing, go get the fire and put it back in it's place. We don't need a pretty brand, we need a GLORY brand. GO GET THE ARK!

MANIFESTING WONDERS.

I AM THE RESSURECTION…He that believeth in Me, thou he were dead, yet shall he live.
-John 11:25

He shewed himself alive after his passion by many infallible proofs, being seen of them forty days, and speaking of the things pertaining to the kingdom of God
-Acts 1:3

I started to get this thing. It started to become alive in me. After the mandate came to get the ark, He gave instructions on what to do with it. The anointing always comes with an assignment. He doesn't just "anoint" you and give you gifts for no reason. Jesus said it best, "the spirit of the Lord is upon me, (why?) He has anointed me to preach the gospel…etc." (Luke 4:18) If your power only works for you, then it's not power. I started to examine all of what I desired to do, and had an honest conversation with myself as to why I wanted to do them.

He spoke to me and He said, "When you go get this glory and bring it back, it's not so that men can say how awesome you are, or how incredible you are. But I want them to see me through you. I want you to tell the world that I'M ALIVE!" He plainly said, "I AM THE RESSURECTION." Now, I know the bible story here, and have been in Sunday school for a good deal of my childhood, so I knew what He was referencing according to scripture. But He said it again, "I AM THE

RESSURECTION." The Resurrection has a personality, He has a mission, a heart, and weight. His mission is simple, to make dead things alive again.

One Sunday, preparing to minister, Holy Spirit spoke early in the morning as I was getting dressed. Often, before I minister, I ask the Lord, what's His agenda for the day? What would He like? I like to ask Him a few questions, after all…it's HIS moment. He didn't speak much then. But as I continued preparing for service, mediating on a few scriptures. He said, "I want to show Myself alive to the people." I wasn't too sure of what He was attempting to make me to know.

Holy Spirit spoke again, and said, "I want you to make yourself as an empty vessel, that I can fill, and use. I desire to walk through the earth, and heal the sick. I want to raise the dead and do mighty exploits, and I want to do it through you. But you have to have no will of your own. If you're going to do it, it has to be done MY WAY."

That's it. It's that simple. This SAME Jesus that

walked through walls, stood in the middle of the sea, calmed and spoke to the winds, wants to do that and more through empty vessels.

There is a secret to the anointing. There is a secret to accessing power. The secret to revival is simply: SURRENDER. We are on the brink of something incredible. There are waves and rivers of GLORY rising at epic proportions. It's readily available for those that will abandon the mundane and go diving for MORE.

There MUST be more. I prophesy that we will see habitations of GLORY throughout the land. GLORY HOUSES and places where people can come just to encounter HIM will become more frequent. I see a culture rising where people irrespective of churches, denominational backgrounds, and race will gather to simply pursing HIM in purity. No agenda, and no fanfare. We are coming into an age of great demonstration. As the world grows dim, pressure will be placed upon the righteous to arise.

He's looking for a vessel. I saw dead men walking on fire. Zombies that had literally come back from the dead, being completely controlled by The Holy Spirit. Men without recognition engulfed in flames. I can't tell you what anyone of them looked like. I can't describe their eyes, and can't tell you how big their noses were. All I know was these human beings were on FIRE.

Strangely enough, while on fire, they were standing in the middle of a river. Amazed, but the water didn't consume the flames. Both the flood and the fire were unlocked. Two seasons became one, and an abiity to withstand multiple seasons were evident. Another thing I noticed was the sound of their marching. As they marched in the river, you could hear the sound of their feet in the water. They were marching and the sound of their steps was a sound of DELIVERANCE. He said unto me, "The burning ones have come to make war and bring NEW, NOW!"

NO male or female. No black church or white. The

next wave of glory bearers will be those of no reputation. They won't be those who have a name or are attempting to make a name for themselves. The uprise will be for the unknown. The common man will walk in unusual glory and demonstration. It will be so, that these will be liken to those that people will ask, "who are these men…and where did they come from?" I do believe HEAVEN has marked a remnant and will respond, "these are they that will unlock God in the earth. These that have come have turned cities upside down. THESE are they that are given for times of DELIVERANCE."

MIRACLES. SIGNS. WONDERS. May the hunger be stirred, the fire be kindled, and may you never settle for a normal Christianity anymore. It's time for REVIVAL!!

Experience a
Personal Holy Revival

Conceived during the year of consecration, God spoke concerning government, politics, the economic structure, and the future of the church. Embark on this prophetic journey. Be ignited and be empowered to walk in the same power as Jesus and even greater. Remarks by Dr. T.L. Lowery.

FREEDOM WARS

FREEDOM WARS is deliverance like you've never seen it before. Dubbed the 2017 "Indie Bestseller" from its distributor, FW explores the process of deliverance from soul-ties and a dysfunctional soul. We journey on the beat skipping, out of sync rhythms, and distressing patterns of the soul. FREEDOM WARS offers deliverance to the deliverer and ministers to the soul of the minister.

J. J. Allen
Foreword By: Sophia Ruffin

XILIX

Eleven Fifty Nine is the song of redemption. Sometimes the greatest dreamers must first live through the worst nightmares. Night seasons are apart of life. It's only when we explore the dark, face our demons, and survive the night, that we can truly embrace the power of the morning.

dedication

One day, scrolling social media, I came across the livestream of this young guy I kept hearing about name, Pastor Shamond Scales. He was leading his church in an intense time of intercession. What got my attention was that for one solid hour, he laid across his stage, and sat upon the steps periodically and just PRAYED! I was hooked from that day. I jokingly call him, my "MOSES". His ministry is often the deliverance God sends to this deliverer! I'm a student of his fellowship with God. REVIVAL is Shamond. The heart, the sound, the grace…he's the fruit of our forefathers in Pentecost's labor! Love you man!!

about the author

J.J. Allen is a fresh prophetic voice. A revivalist, independent film-maker, and writer. With humor, honesty, and passion he challenges head-on spiritually and socially flawed perspectives. He's the founder of The HEARTBEAT Brand, a thriving organism that reintroduces authentic spirituality.

www.hbbrand.me